GOD MADE THAT FIRST!

Written By Angela Metts

Dedicated to my Dad~

With sincere joy, I dedicate this book to You Daddy God. It is only right that my first book be about You! Thank You for loving me. I was a terrified little girl and You saved me. Over and over You save me. Thank You! A zillion times a zillion, Thank You! You are my life, my hope, and my love. You are my everything! You make me brave! Help me to trust You more and more. And one day call me home to You. Until that longed for day help me do all that is in Your heart here. My greatest joy is You. This book is for You. All credit and honor is Yours, for You are the giver of every good gift. Thank You for sharing Your thoughts with me, thank You for being You. I pray Father, that each reader may feel Your very presence and awesome love as they turn these pages. May they come to know You as close as I have, and even more so! I love You, always and forever.

~Love, Your daughter
Angela

Special Thanks~

Special and great thanks to my faithful friend and husband Jamie. Your love has transformed my life! Thank you to my beautiful children; truly, you are one of God's most precious and amazing gifts to me. To my Blessed Grand Children, I hope you fall in love with God and find Him everywhere! Thank you to all my God sent friends and family who have encouraged me to write for many years. And to the God placed parents who have labored to love and pray me through life's most broken paths, my heart is forever and eternally thankful. Thank you for your love, for it changed me and on the darkest days brought rays of light. I love each of you, always and forever...

~ Love, Angela

A Letter to you~

Dear Reader,

    It is my honor to present this humble book. God began to reveal the following contents to me over the past few years. He so graciously allowed me to find Him everywhere. I found Him in His generosity with the sun, moon, and stars. I found Him in His faithfulness in the night. I found His desire for closeness to mankind in the garden with Adam and Eve. I found my enormous all-powerful God closer than I had ever imagined. Everywhere I look, there He is! My heart is to share what He has so tenderly shared with me. My hope is that you will find Him and fall in love as I have. He is vastly beyond my small understanding yet He allows me to know Him so simply. God loves you. All creation testifies to His profound faithful love. His love for you is more than you can ever dream!

Love Always,
Angela

For since the creation of the world God's invisible qualities-His eternal power and divine nature-have been clearly seen, being understood from what has been made, so that people are without excuse. Romans 1:20 NIV

Table of contents

Author's Dedication & Special Thanks iii

A Letter to you v

Chapter 1: The 1st Light 2

Chapter 2: The 1st Night Light 6

Chapter 3: The 1st Surgeon and the 1st Anesthesiologist! 10

Chapter 4: The 1st Garden 14

Chapter 5: The 1st Zoo 22

Chapter 6: The 1st Tailor 28

Chapter 7: The 1st Artist 36

Chapter 8: The 1st Aquarium 40

Chapter 9: The 1st Swimming Pool 44

Chapter 10: The 1st Water Sprinkler and Shower 48

Chapter 11: The 1st Fan 52

Chapter 12: The 1st Rainbow 56

Psalm 104 60

Closing 64

GOD MADE THAT FIRST!

BY ANGELA METTS

Chapter 1
The 1st Light

By A. Metts. Meet Freedom, his eyes are blue, his gait is soft, and I'm in awe of God's creation!

The 1st Light

One afternoon I was walking through a beautiful gathering of tall green pine trees when I heard God's gentle voice.

"Where does the sunlight go?"

His question stirred my heart in excitement. I began to study my surroundings. Following the scattered sunrays through the forest, my eyes found the end of one ray after another. One ray brazenly chased through the trees until it found the blockade of an old rotten stump. There it warmed the chipping old wood on the front side while leaving the stump's backside dark and wanting. One ray peaked through the makings of an elaborate spider web causing slivers of it to shine like glistening silver. Another ray fell confidently on the barren ground, shining as if it were soon to be a great garden; another on nearby beautiful wild flowers and perfect bunches of grass. One sunray lay even across the sadly discarded and twisted plastic bottle. Other rays did not flinch at resting on the rusty barbed wire fence, nor did the sun's rays shine brighter once they found the back of my flashy black and white paint horse. The rays seemed to love all they touched wholeheartedly.

"What is it You want me to see Lord?" I asked in return to His question.

"See how generous I am with the sun? It shows no favoritism or partiality. It shines through the window of the rich man's house just as it shines through the window of the poor man's house. The sun shines on the face of an evil person just as it shines on the face of a righteous one. The sun is massive yet humble. It graces the highest places on earth yet gracefully lights the lowest as well. A lot is to be learned by My sun."

His steady voice and great wisdom astounded me. In awe, my eyes continued to search out the sun's rays. In my heart, I finally spoke to Him.

"You are so generous Lord, so generous and so profoundly powerful."

I sensed Him smiling at my awareness of Him.

Let us look at this first light ever created, God's amazing sun. Did you know that over a million earths could fit inside of the sun? Now that is a tremendously huge light! The sun is not only the first light ever created but the sun's light also divides the day from the night making it possible to keep time. The sun was one of the first clocks and calendars. The sun was used to keep track of days, years, and seasons. The sun is an astounding light that continues to rise each morning without a switch! Then every evening the sun slowly dims as the earth rotates. This glorious sun goes down each evening sharing its light with the other side of the earth.

Do you have a light that shares? I do not! Lol! (laugh out loud). The sunlight benefits our entire planet! There are still many places on earth without manmade lights. These places rely on God's timely and generous sun every day. I am so very thankful for God's sun and that He never sends any of us a light bill! His light bulb never goes out or requires changing! I reckon He knew it would be fruitless for us to design a stepladder tall enough. How unselfish and faithfully generous of Him to give us the sun!

Life in any form could not exist on earth without the sun! The sun brings life giving warmth on cold wintry days. It can thaw the ice and snow off massive mountains. The sun helps all plants and animals grow. The sun has health benefits for people as well. When a person spends the right amount of time in the sun, their skin will produce the very needful vitamin D. Who knew one huge light has so many benefits? In fact, there are many more benefits that are not listed. God's magnificent sun is the first and greatest of all lights on earth!

Fresh hope releases as the sun rises each morning declaring a new day. As the sun's rays kiss you, pause just for a moment and feel its great warmth. Ponder God's gloriously lit masterpiece.

And God said, "Let there be lights in the expanse of the heavens to separate the day from the night. And let them be for signs and for seasons, and for days and years, Genesis 1:14 ESV

To Him who made the great lights, for His steadfast love endures forever; The sun to rule over the day, for His steadfast love endures forever; Psalm 136:7-8 ESV

Chapter 2
The 1st Night Light

By A. Metts. A picture of the moon I took one night.

The 1st Night Light

Who is the 1st night light maker? Great question! God made the very first night lights. He made the beautiful stars and the amazing moon!

> (God made) the moon and stars to govern the night; His love endures forever. Psalm 139:12

God so generously offers beautiful stars and this ever-changing moon without a monthly bill and without prejudice. You do not have to be good or bad to have His night light. It is free! You do not have to remember to turn this night light on. There are one hundred billion stars in a single galaxy. Now that is a lot of nightlights! When God makes something, He sure goes above and beyond!

Let us move on to our largest night light, the moon. The moon's average distance from earth is a whopping two hundred thirty eight thousand, eight hundred and fifty seven miles. Wow! Now the moon has to be a bright light to shine through that many miles. Night after night, God is faithful, His bright stars and His riveting moon continue to shine without our help at all. This is amazing!

There may be rare nights, however, the stars and moon are difficult to see. They are still in the sky but their light is hidden behind many clouds or a big storm. This might be similar to a person standing in front of your night light at home. As soon as this person moves away from the night light then the light shines bright again! So be patient, when the storm is over the stars and moon will shine again. Another amazing quality about

God and the night is that He can see through the dark. That is right, God sees through the night as if it were day!

> Even the darkness is not dark to You; the night is bright as the day, for darkness is as light with You. Psalm 139:12 ESV

> This is the message we heard from Him and proclaim to you, that God is light, and in Him is no darkness in Him at all. 1 John 1:5 ESV

> Nothing in all creation is hidden from God's sight. Everything is uncovered and laid bare before the eyes of Him to Whom we must give account. Hebrews 4:13 NIV

Wow! God is light! Nothing can hide from God. Knowing He sees in the dark makes me brave! Remember next time it is dark and you may be feeling fearful to trust in God and His power. He is the greatest light ever! He is with us!

It was not too long ago I was afraid of the dark. Something terrible happened in my life and sudden tormenting thoughts would wait for me when I stepped into the black night. The definition of fear helped me understand it better. There are two types of fear. One fear is good and the other is evil. The good fear is a reverent respect held for God. This good fear is a feeling of awe and respect of His amazing presence and power. There is no torment in the good fear. The second fear is a painful feeling that expects something evil to happen. This evil fear has torment causing pain, suffering, distress, and more. We are talking about the evil fear for now. The opposite of evil fear in my opinion is faith. Faith expects something good to happen.

Using myself as an example, when I would walk outside into the dark and terrible thoughts began to enter my mind, my body would be afraid as I thought about scary thoughts. Sometimes a nervous sweat would moisten my skin and my heart would beat rapidly. This was a terrible feeling that I permitted for months until I did some research. God showed me His power over the dark and my thoughts began to change. He said the night is as bright as day to Him! Learning that He can see through the dark caused me to have faith, to expect something good. Now, when I step into the dark I imagine God's excellent vision seeing everything! I feel peace because I trust God and pray before I go anywhere. Did you know that it says do not fear in the Bible three hundred and sixty five times? Wow, that is once for every day of the year! God does not want us to have evil fear. In fact, here is one of my favorite scriptures about fear.

> There is no fear in love. But perfect love drives out fear, because fear has to do with punishment. The one who fears is not made perfect in love. 1 John 4:18 NIV

God loves us all perfectly. His love drives out evil fear. Focus on God's love for you and watch the amazing change! Next time you gaze out into the dark and see the beautiful stars or the soft moonlight, remember God turned His splendid night lights on for you. Oh, how He loves you!

Chapter 3
The 1ˢᵗ Surgeon and the 1ˢᵗ Anesthesiologist!

See the joy when two people meet and fall in love! Meet my amazing brother and his gorgeous wife, representing God's profound creation of mankind!

The 1st Anesthesiologist and the 1st Surgeon!

Did you know that God was the first Anesthesiologist and the first Surgeon? Wow! What is an anesthesiologist? What is a surgeon? Those are both great questions! An anesthesiologist gives the patient with the broken bone enough medicine to fall asleep and not feel any pain while the surgeon is operating on the patient. Now for the surgeon, a surgeon is a medical doctor who operates or (cuts open) a patient to fix something that is broken inside of them. A good example might be a surgeon cutting open a person's arm to fix a broken bone.

In Genesis 2:21-22 it tells us that God caused Adam to fall into a deep sleep and He then took one of Adams ribs out to make Eve. God, long before there was a first doctor on earth showed us just how a doctor should be. First, He loved His patient. Second, He saw a great need in Adam and waited for Adam to recognize that need. God then followed His perfect plan to meet that need at Adam's request. God did not want Adam to hurt so He put Adam into a deep sleep and while he was sleeping cut out one of his ribs to form Eve. He then closed Adam's cut. Adam was amazed when he woke up! I do not think he has ever missed his rib. He loved his wife and friend, Eve, so much!

How touching it is to know, that God can look deep within us and immediately know what we need. How patient He is waiting for us to see our need of Him. Even greater are His thoughts and intents to meet that need if we allow Him. God is definitely our perfect Surgeon and Anesthesiologist! How amazing and profoundly wise God is. Many doctors, nurses, and medical staff pray today and ask God for wisdom to help them when they operate or perform procedures for patients. God is generous in perfect examples and giving us wisdom when we ask.

The 1st Surgeon and the 1st Anesthesiologist!

And the LORD God caused the man to fall into a deep sleep; and while he was sleeping, He took one of the man's ribs and then closed up the place of the flesh. Then the LORD God made a woman from the rib He had taken out of the man, and He brought her to the man.
Genesis 2:21-22 NIV

If any of you lacks wisdom, you should ask God, who gives generously to all without finding fault, and it will be given to you. James 1:5 NIV

Chapter 4
The 1st Garden

By A. Metts. A rose without thorns, imagine that garden!

The 1st Garden

The first garden is one not only I, but many people have earnestly longed for. This garden existed back when briars and thorns did not. Poisonous ivies and allergies were nonexistent. This garden was perfect, for God designed and planted it. Large fragrant roses of great beauty sang soft melodies with long smooth stems. Multicolored wild flowers danced upon open fields in perfect sequence. Full trees draped overhead hanging with delicious unmarred fruits. Sweet fragrances permeated the entire garden. A beautiful huge river ran through its scenic grounds.

Here in this garden God walked every day with Adam. This garden is the Garden of Eden. Here, God brought the many animals He created to Adam and asked Adam to name each one. Can you imagine for a moment Adam's excitement or admiration of God? What were their conversations? When Adam tasted the different fruits, did he and God discuss God's sole purpose of each? Did Adam express his opinion and pick favorites? Did Adam ask God His thoughts when He made the huge elephant's trunk or the perfect fun stripes of the zebra? Did they laugh and celebrate God's genius creativity? Did Adam study each plant and ask what its purpose was or how to grow it? Did he greatly admire the mighty sequoia tree? Or, bask smiling in the beauty of the inspiring Japanese Maple?

I believe God was showing His immense understanding and vast wisdom to Adam through His creation. God was sharing Himself. After all, it is no fun if you do not have someone you love to share your greatest work! I imagine they laughed together and rejoiced over all God made. Soon after the animals were named, Adam realized he did not have a mate. God saw a need in Adam and answered. God created beautiful Eve and she too walked with them in this immense garden. Father God loved His time with them both. Day after day, He faithfully returned at the same time to walk and talk with them.

Imagine for a moment, that God himself plants you an amazing garden and He comes over at the same time every day just to be with you! Whoa! I would be coming to your garden for sure! Yes!

The first garden was heavenly, perfect, and full of joy in the presence of Almighty God! Here in this abundant garden He made man and woman in His own image. God blessed Adam and Eve in this amazing garden. He gave them dominion, the skill and wisdom to work and keep this gorgeous garden. He gave them specific instructions to live a wonderful life with Him here.

God commanded Adam that he and Eve could eat of every tree but do not eat off the tree of good and evil for if they did, they would surely die. Sometime later Eve began to listen to an unfamiliar voice in the garden. This voice was not her devoted God's; nor was it the voice or her loving husband, Adam's voice. This voice belonged to her enemy! In disguise, he whispered evil deceptive words mixed with truth and doubt. Eve allowed the enemy's deceiving words in and did not resist them.

Her enemy was the devil who hated and betrayed God. His lethal plan was to steal the power God had given to Adam and

Eve and kill them. Bringing death to them was killing two precious pieces of God. His motive; to slay God in every possible way, so that he himself would be god. In all honesty, the devil must be utterly deceived for he must have forgotten Who made him. To think he could ever be more powerful than God is completely ignorant. Have you ever seen a tool outsmart the toolmaker? No. My point exactly.

Eve, to all creations cringe took of the fruit that day. Adam, who also knew of God's command, willingly chose to listen to Eve's voice and ate the forbidden fruit too. Instantly, both Adam and Eve felt the power of deadly sin and heavy shame for the first time ever. Their physical eyes were all they could see through now. Their sins brought spiritual death separating them from the presence of their loving God. Fear and doubt by legal right entered the garden and clung tormenting them.

When God came to walk and talk with them, they were hiding because they were afraid. God knew what they both had done but called to them as He had faithfully had done so many times before. Oh, how God loved them! All knowing God asked them what happened like any balanced parent. Patiently, He listened as Adam and Eve each told their side of the story. There were devastating effects due to the sowing of sin. God explained that they could no longer live in the Garden of Eden. That both Adam and Eve would experience pains and labors they had not yet known.

God in His compassion and mercy knew Adam and Eve were scared and aware of their nakedness. He made them both clothes even after they had chosen to believe the enemies lies over His loving true command. That day, the Garden of Eden was void of earths favored family. The garden lost its long time and joyous stewards, and Adam and Eve were sent to live outside of its beloved haven. Death had been birthed into all creation. Thorns and other dark things began to manifest. Earth must have grieved. However, God had a plan.

The LORD God planted a garden eastward in Eden, and there He put the man who He had formed. And out of the ground the LORD God made every tree grow that is pleasant to the sight and good for food. The tree of life was also in the middle of the garden, and the tree of the knowledge of good and evil. Genesis 2:8-9 KJV

So God created mankind in His own image, in the image of God He created them; male and female He created them. God blessed them and said to them, "Be fruitful and increase in number; fill the earth and subdue it. Rule over the fish in the sea and the birds in the sky and over every living creature that moves on the ground." Genesis 1:27-28 NIV

God is extravagant in all He does; see how He made trees that were good for food and trees that were also pleasant to the sight? God is not cheap but rather extravagant. He definitely goes over and above anything we can imagine! Awe, and to be made in His image...what an honor.

We all can learn a lot from this garden. What voice are you listening to? Is it a voice that mocks God or sows doubt? Or, do you hear your heavenly Father's loving voice? We must pay close attention to who is talking to us. It is often a simple lousy or deceptive thought that leads to making one bad decision.

It was while writing this very chapter on the first garden when the Lord impressed my heart with a new garden. I had felt Adam and Eve were able to experience God in ways that I had so desired. I was jealous of their time and experience with God. I longed to walk and talk with God like them!

Then the Lord revealed that His Son Jesus died and rose again to bring each of us back to our own garden with God. Through Jesus, we receive forgiveness of our sins and are made right with God! Yes, we can walk and talk with God. Hallelujah! This garden is in the spirit realm. In this magnificent garden, the Father is with us... not just at a certain time... but all the time! All because Jesus died and took all the power back from our enemy the devil. Jesus restored us to our Father God and gave us back the very power the devil stole that day in the Garden of Eden. Thank You Jesus!

We enter this sacred garden every day in our relationship with God. This secret garden's gate is unlocked through Jesus, God's Son. Oh, the joy that awaits us in the garden!

For God so loved the world that He gave His one and only Son, that whoever believes in Him shall not perish, but have eternal life.

John 3:16 NIV

Prayer being so much more than asking, but also thanking God, waiting and listening for His response. Too many of us fear God will not answer, so we make our requests and rush to the Amen. This is like calling your dad and saying "Dad, will you bring me dinner?" and then suddenly hanging up. Hanging up like that would hurt your earthly father deeply. How much more your heavenly Father loves you and longs to speak to you. Prayer is bonding time, it is learning to hear His voice, it is where His presence is great, and joy is full! It is a real relationship filled with questions, answers, correction, worship and so much more.

This relationship with our heavenly Father possesses every emotion we have as people. When we are sad, we can talk to Him and reveal our broken heart. When we are happy, we can share with Him the day's joy and victories. When we have questions, we can ask Him. When we fail miserably, we can run to Him and ask forgiveness. When our burdens from life are weighing us down, we can ask Him to take them. Have you ever-asked God if He was angry, sad, or happy? Or, asked Him if there was something He would like you to pray about? Has He ever touched your heart and gently corrected you? Or does He nudge you to go apologize to someone? Amazing things happen in this garden of our hearts! You see, we can spend time with God here in this secret place anytime and anywhere. How wonderfully profound! This garden is yours and yours alone.

For if, because of one man's trespass, death reigned through that one man, much more will those who receive the abundance of grace and the free gift of righteousness reign in life through the one man Jesus Christ. Romans 5:17 ESV

People often wonder why there is still so much evil present on earth. In my humble opinion, the above scripture gives us insight. That those people who receive the free gift of righteousness from Jesus will reign in life through Christ. To reign in Christ would be to live on earth according to God's word and principal. Jesus overcame evil with good. He gave His own life so that we could be healed and restored. God reigns in truth and love. However, who is reigning in the people who have not received our loving savior? You see the earth will one day be rid of the devil but for now, he is present in this world until his eternal damnation.

If your heart longs for God, believe John 3:16 that God so loves you that He gave His only Son Jesus to die so that you will have eternal life with Him.

Chapter 5
The 1st Zoo

Meet Joy! She has been with us for over ten years. She still runs to greet us, but she now sits when we ask her to! Lol!

Pictures by A. Metts

The 1st Zoo

Who created the very first Zoo? God, that's Who! What is your favorite animal? Is it the horse? Is it the cat? Or is it the dog? Scientist guess there are about one to two million different species of animals on earth. There are animals I have not even seen yet! After looking up a few odd animals on the internet, here is what I learned.

Did you know there is such an animal called the Pink fairy armadillo, or the Raspberry crazy ant, or Star nosed mole? God is just too much for me! He again has gone over and above. His creative beauty is seen in the stately feathered peacock. His great patterns of design in the perfectly striped Zebra. His amazing Lion displays strength and courage. His sheep example the true need of a shepherd. The eagle teaches us to fly above the storms of life. The snake has taught us the trickery of deception. The dove has taught us true gentleness. The first trash service can be seen in the vulture's duty. Often I have witnessed them picking up dead things by the road. By the ant, He teaches us wisdom. The very first camo is brilliantly displayed upon the elusive leopard and many other creatures. God's camouflage has no equal.

The inner workings of muscle and bone and all that makes these animals move will astound even the greatest scholar. Understand this; the Creator who designed each animal has left a tremendous message imbedded for us to search out. God knows and understands the traits He placed in each animal. There is no end to His infinite wisdom! So study those animals a little closer for you may unveil more mysteries and insight.

And God said, "Let the earth bring forth living creatures according to their kinds-livestock and creeping things and beasts of the earth according to their kinds." And it was so. God made the beasts of the earth according to their kinds and the livestock according to their kinds, and everything that creeps on the ground according to its kind. And God saw that it was good.
Genesis 1:24-25 ESV

Look at the birds of the air; they do not sow or reap or store away in barns, and yet your heavenly Father feeds them. Are you not much more valuable than they? Matthew 6:26 NIV

Go to the ant, you sluggard; consider its ways and be wise!
Proverbs 6:6-8 NIV

Allow me to share with you two animals my family and I have been so blessed to own. The first animal is a drab gray dog that showed up on our property. Joyfully she ran down our driveway as if she lived there and our family had not received the memo yet. Having chickens that roamed freely in our yard I sternly ran her off. She would turn and trot just out of sight and then run merrily back. Stubbornly, I ran her off several more times. Still, as if she had received some secret mail label with our address, she more stubbornly and still happily returned! My sweet niece who knew of the recent passing of my beloved half wolf named Dowboy calmly smiled and spoke.

"Aunt, I believe God sent you a dog." She said with a hopeful smile.

"I don't want another dog right now." Painfully, I replied.

Deep down I just didn't have the hope of ever finding another Dowboy. I had raised him from a small puppy after his mom had died. He and I had walked and jogged countless miles together. When I was sad, I would sit silently on the front porch and he would sit next to me. He seemed to sense my moods. Eventually my unnatural silence would get the best of him and he would so cleverly place his paw on my arm. Turning to look at him my smile would eat away the sorrow, and for a moment, all was well.

Fourteen years I had his faithful friendship. Dowboy was with our family through divorce, marriage, the wonderful entry of all our children, deaths, through seven moves, the ups the downs of our life and still he chose to stay. He was my friend, the one who never asked questions and always wanted to see me. One cold January evening we found Dowboy leaning next to my car. His breathing was shallow, and in my heart, I knew he was about to die. I felt the close of our time together as I held him. Gently petting his loyal face, I thanked him for his years of friendship and love. I told him he did well in this life and he would love heaven. It was then that I could feel the weighty value of his friendship. We buried him with my favorite running shirt in a coffin like box the vet had given us. We thanked God for all our years and joy with him. Our whole family cried when Dowboy died.

Although I knew, he was happy in heaven, my legs had no want to walk, and my knees had no desire to bend. The road seemed too lonely to walk without him. Months would pass before I would go walking again. Meanwhile, this drab gray dog kept returning and my niece kept repeating...

"Aunt, God sent you a dog."

Suddenly wagging out of control, she knocked my two small children down! Aggravated, I raised my voice and told the dog to sit as I reached to help my son and daughter to their feet. The dog knew of no such command and continued to joyously wag her tail and greet us.

"That's it! I am going to teach you how to sit and find you a home!" I spouted in an irritated but determined tone.

That was nearly ten years ago. I taught her how to sit and she did find a home. Our home! Somehow, she won our hearts! Of course, her placing her paw on my arm one afternoon wrecked me in her favor! We named her Joy, this name seemed so fitting as her happiness in meeting, and greeting us has never waned. Still after ten years, she bounds down the driveway overjoyed to see us! She too has been one of the most loyal and smart dogs we have owned to date.

There are times when joy comes wrapped in drab gray packages that we never intend to unwrap. Sometimes, God really does send you a dog, or maybe even more than one. Never stop hoping. Never stop believing. Dare to unwrap those gray packages! Dare to love again, it makes life worth living.

I shared this true story to give insight to just one of Gods many animals. How generous of the Lord to make an animal that is loyal and protective by nature. How calming to run ones hand down their furry back. How fun they are to run and play with! How comforting it is, they never tire to see us.

God is genius and so generous in creation! Thank You God for sending us Joy!

The 1st Zoo

God's Zoo

Lions, tigers, and big, big bears!
Horses, and dogs and monkeys that stare!
Dinosaurs, elephants, rhinos and more!
Rabbits, kittens, and critters galore!
Birds of all feathers that chirp and sing!
Oceans deep with innumerable things!
Take time to study, searching here or there.
Oh, be ready to find God everywhere!
Great You are God! Magnificent and profound!
Your unfailing love and faithful heart in all creation found!
We are in awe of You, Creator of this great earth!
Designer of galaxies and creations birth!

By Angela Metts

Chapter 6
The 1ˢᵗ Tailor

By A. Metts. I asked God what picture could represent Adam and Eve and Him clothing them. I saw this picture so clearly in my heart. These hands represent God handing the perfect clothes He made to Adam and Eve. Look closer, this picture is worth a thousand words!

The 1st Tailor

A person who sews clothes is a tailor. A person somewhere sewed the very clothes you are wearing right now! So... guess who might be the very first Tailor? You guessed right! Genesis 3:21 tells us that God made both Adam and Eve's clothes from animal skins. I never imagined God making clothes, but He did. He cared so much for Adam and Eve. He cares so much for you and I. For God to make Adam and Eve's clothes He had to come very close to them. Close enough to know what size each of them were. Details like shirt size, waist size, pant size, even the length of their legs and arms. Never once did He speak negatively on their size. Adam and Eve had just disobeyed God, still He made them clothes.

How would you like God to come over and make you some clothes? Imagine Him close enough to measure you. Of course, in His supreme intelligence He would not need a tape measure. One look from Him and He would know all that is necessary. Wow, I bet the clothes He made would be the coolest clothes ever! God's clothes would fit perfectly too. God has never made a single mistake! I smile at this thought for if the God who made our amazing creation and breath-taking galaxies is humble enough to come so close and make clothes, how I long to know Him more!

The LORD God made garments of skin for Adam and his wife and clothed them. Genesis 3:21 NIV

For I know the plans I have for you," declares the LORD, "plans to prosper you and not to harm you, plans to give you hope and a future. Jeremiah 29:11 NIV

The God who made the world and everything in it, being Lord of heaven and earth, does not live in temples made by man, nor is He served by human hands, as though He needed anything, since He himself gives to all mankind life and breath and everything. And He made from one man every nation of mankind to live on all the face of the earth, having determined allotted periods and the boundaries of their dwelling place, that they should seek God, and perhaps feel their way toward Him and find Him. Yet He is actually not far from each one of us. Acts 17:24-37 ESV

My heart is so moved by this verse... that we should seek God and feel our way toward Him and find Him. Yet He is actually not far from each one of us. How comforting to know He is not far and that if we choose to seek God we will find Him.

I was eight when I sought God. I was eight when I found God! Child protective services had removed me and three other siblings from my mother. There was no foster home to take us in at the time so my older sister Tammy took the necessary classes so she could raise us. Tammy had three beautiful children of her own making a grand total of seven. She was brave to take on four broken abused and neglected children.

Tammy took us to church and it was there, my life changed forever. (Thank you, Tammy. I love you and am eternally thankful!) The pastor at that little church talked of how God was a Father to those who had no father. He talked of how much God loved children, that God never lied and always kept His promises. A love I had never experienced flowed from this pastor. In awe, I listened for I had longed for a dad so deeply. The pastor asked if anyone wanted to invite God into their heart that day. Raising my small hand up into the air, my heart quickly raced. Tightly squeezing my eyes shut I repeated the sinner's prayer following the pastors words. Hope instantly filled my heart! An unknown excitement enveloped me. Just then, I felt someone hold my hand. Quickly opening my eyes to see who it was, I saw no one. All I knew was suddenly I felt an amazing peace I had never known and I had a Dad... the Dad... Daddy God! And this Dad would never leave me! I was in heaven on earth!

Naturally, I just began to talk with God, sharing my fears and telling Him over and over how much I loved Him! So childish, yet so pure were our talks. Later I would learn the great need for being childlike and loving God so transparently. How simple prayer really is. Lying on the bottom of the bunkbed in my room one day, I asked God a hard question.

"God, where did I come from? Because I don't feel like I came from my mother."

My eyes traced a lovely picture that hung on the wall to my right as I paused waiting for His answer. I hated the broken feeling when I thought of my mom. The abuse had driven us apart.

Suddenly I was in the throne room of God! I had never read the Bible or had time to learn about the throne room but even at eight years of age I knew it was the throne room of God Almighty! There is a knowing in the presence of God. The most marvelous love filled the air and you could breathe it! Great peace was everywhere as my spirit flew counter clockwise around God with great joy! There was no question of His authority or power for they both were equally present. Many other spirits flew with me. We loved God with all our beings. Our spirits were like beautiful lightning streaks with immeasurable jubilation. With the greatest joy we whirled about God's throne over and over in worship! Then God spoke.

"Whom shall I send? Whom shall I send? Who will go for Me?"

His voice was permeating with perfect clarity. His voice possessed utter victory. With everything within me and my full will I answered Him with astounding joy and determination!

"Send me Lord, I'll go! Send me Lord, I'll go!"

My voice was loud and eager as I flew once more past His throne. Joy cannot begin to describe the height or depth of happiness I felt at that moment! Great delight and sheer jubilee dare come close.

Suddenly, I was back on the bottom bunk bed. In awe, I laid there silent, not yet fully able to understand all it meant. I told no one but hid it in my heart. Still, after forty-three years on earth, nothing compares to this encounter and I have never forgotten it. There is a knowing inside of me that God's answer to my question that day is a marvelous gift. I'm still in awe that God spoke to me, a broken little girl that wasn't worth anything to most people. He knew the abuse I had endured had wounded the natural mother daughter bond and left me feeling abandoned.

God never put my mother down nor did He batter my earthly dad, He simply showed me how great He is! There is no "if" with God. There is no "maybe", or "could have been", or He "might" find me on earth after He sent me. He never tore my earthly parents down to build Himself up. God is victory, complete and total victory! God knows who He is, even when we doubt. That day in His throne room, He knew He would find me on earth no matter who my parents might be. He reached for me that day at church and I reached back. How profoundly beautiful. How many people push Him away? Reach for Him… He is reaching out to you now.

Time passed into adulthood and the Lord would reveal His precious gift even more to me over time. He showed me that all life comes from Him.

All things were made through Him, and without Him was not anything made that was made. In Him was life, and the life was the light of men. John 1:3-4 ESV

Father of the fatherless and protector of widows is God in his holy habitation. Psalm 68:5 ESV

For You formed my inward parts; You knitted me together in my mother's womb. I praise You, for I am fearfully and wonderfully made. Wonderful are Your works; my soul knows it very well. Psalm 139:13-14 ESV

God Made That First!

> Thus says God, the LORD, who created the heavens and stretched them out, who spread out the earth and what comes from it, who gives breath to the people on it and spirit to those who walk in it:
> Isaiah 42:5 ESV

God revealed that my parents were my gate into this earth, but my life came from Him. My parents came from Him too; they just did not know it yet. He asked me to forgive my parents. They too were broken and in turn caused pain to others. He taught me to honor and love them just the way they were. In forgiving them, I was free to be like my heavenly Father. Finally, I was free from the abandonment, the abuse, the neglect, and the pain.

You can be free too. God does not show favoritism. God wishes that none would perish. Ask and believe God to come into your life today.

> The Lord is not slow to fulfill his promise as some count slowness, but is patient toward you, not wishing that any should perish, but that all should reach repentance. 2 Peter 3:9 ESV

> If you confess with your mouth that Jesus is Lord and believe in your heart that God raised him from the dead, you will be saved.
> Romans 10:9-10 ESV

> For if you forgive others their trespasses, your heavenly Father will also forgive you, but if you do not forgive others their trespasses, neither will your Father forgive your trespasses.
> Matthew 6:14-15 ESV

God restored my relationship with my mother and father as the years passed. Both of them asked Jesus to be Lord of their lives. This journey was not without pain or longsuffering but worth it in the end. There are definitely some intriguing chapters for another day and another book. <3

Chapter 7
The 1st Artist

By A. Metts, God's glorious art He so generously painted one morning!

The heavens declare the glory of God; the skies proclaim the work of His hands. Psalm 19:1 NIV

"Lord, our Lord, how majestic is Your name in all the earth! You have set Your glory in the heavens...When I consider Your heavens, the work of Your fingers, the moon and the stars, which You have set in place, what is mankind that You are mindful of them, human beings that You care for them?"
Psalm 8:1, 3-4 NIV

The 1ˢᵗ Artist

In our world, we have many talented artists. Some artists create their art with clay to make sculptures. Other artists draw, paint, design, and weld, the list can go on and on. Yet, no artist on earth creates a new piece faithfully every single day, year after year after year. There is but one Artist in all creation with such vast talent, His name is God. Each morning He paints His skies breathtaking colors amidst whirling white clouds. The light from His sun reflects perfectly on all in its path. His paintings merge or disappear before our very eyes. His powdery clouds gently work themselves off the page. His evening skies are one of my great delights!

God made the first light show too. Have you heard of the great northern lights? These lights are found in both the northern and southern hemispheres. They are like curtains of divine colors dancing in the sky! These heavenly displays can reach the height of 620 miles. Wow!

God's astounding sky masterpieces humbly disappear each day. Faithfully He paints anew! What artist so willingly erases each piece and even so without a bit of recognition? There is no charge for this alluring gallery. The endless sky is His canvas and all creation sings in applause! Truly, He is not only of great generosity but also clothes Himself in the royalty of humility. Each morning we rise to His next great piece. Relentless, He is faithful to continue. His art is profound! Whether He has designed a mesmerizing sunset, the awe-inspiring northern lights, or the lightning lit sky, He takes the grand prize!

The heavens declare the glory of God; the skies proclaim the work of His hands. Psalm 19:1 NIV

Through Him (God) all things were made; without Him nothing was made that has been made. John 1:3 NIV

The 1st Artist

"Lord, our Lord, how majestic is Your name in all the earth! You have set Your glory in the heavens...When I consider Your heavens, the work of Your fingers, the moon and the stars, which You have set in place, what is mankind that You are mindful of them, human beings that You care for them?" Psalm 8:1, 3-4 NIV

Chapter 8
The 1ˢᵗ Aquarium

Pictures by A. Metts. Bottom is a man-made aquarium...

Top picture is three great men fishing in God's vast aquarium!

The 1st Aquarium

Do you have an aquarium? We do not have one but we often go to a local business that has a huge aquarium. This aquarium is filled with so many beautiful fish. My daughter and I love to sit and watch the fish swim back and forth. There are large fish, small fish, skinny fish, fat fish, pink fish, orange fish, fluorescent fish, and there are even funny looking fish. With our world's most amazing manmade aquariums they still pale in comparison to the very first gigantic aquarium!

There are around 228,450 known species in the ocean. It is said that some two million more species are yet to be identified. This total does not include the species in rivers, lakes, or ponds. God's great seas, lakes, rivers, and ponds are the very first aquariums! In fact, every manmade aquarium picked their fish right out of God's aquarium. He sure designs the perfect example for us to follow. We can study the way He places the fish together, the type of water, and the climate so that we can make our own small aquariums! Genius He is, and extremely generous as the total of His creation is still being counted today.

Then God said, "Let the waters abound with an abundance of living creatures, and let the birds fly above the earth across the face of the firmament of the heavens." So, God created great sea creatures and every living thing that moves, with which the waters abounded, according to their kind, and every winged bird according to its kind. And God saw that it was good. Genesis 1:20-21 NKJV

In His hand are the depths of the earth, and the mountain peaks belong to Him. The sea is His, for He made it, and His hands formed the dry land.

Psalm 95:4-5 NIV

The 1st Aquarium

How many are Your works, LORD! In wisdom, You made them all; the earth is full of Your creatures. There is the sea, vast and spacious, teeming with creatures beyond number ~ living things both large and small.

Psalm 104:24-25 NIV

Chapter 9
The 1st Swimming Pool

By A. Metts. Some of my sweet family playing in God's ocean pool!

The 1st Swimming Pool

Fun! Talk about fun in the sun in a nice pool on a hot summer day! Can you hear the kids splashing and laughter filling the air? Our manmade pools are definitely a high note for all of us who love to swim. We have made the salt-water pool to mimic the salty ocean water. We have the chlorine pools filled with special chemicals to kill bacteria and keep the water clear. We have even designed organic pools that are made to filter themselves naturally. Even so, God still made the very first pool! He made the large lake pool. He made the small pool we call the pond. He made the original wave pool called the ocean! LOL and He made the original lazy river but His is not so lazy ha-ha. His pools cross the world and are located in nearly every land!

Once while talking with the Lord in prayer I saw God swim. In a beautiful clear flowing river, He swam with great joy! I was in shock, as I never imagined God swimming. However, I saw Him swim that day. And as He swam making great ripples in the beautiful clear water, He lovingly laughed knowing my thoughts.

"I invented fun Angela!" His voice carried over the waters noise.

In awe, I sat there, on the river's edge atop a large rock. God swims. I smile even now in remembrance!

He knew the pressure of life could be soothed by a sweet summer swim. He knew the joy and life pool-time would bring to so many families. He is the author of fun! I hope you are beginning to see more of God's heart in what He created. He created it all to tell a story about Him. He longs to reveal to the furthest nation His existence, His love, His salvation, the bounty of His generosity. Next time when you go swimming, whether in a manmade pool or the deep blue ocean, I hope you will remember to say thank You Lord! His mercies are new every morning and His love is never-ending for us all.

The 1st Swimming Pool

And God said, "Let the waters below the heavens be gathered together into one place, and let the dry land appear"; And it was so. God called the dry land Earth, and the gathering of the waters He called Seas; and God saw that it was good.
Genesis 1:9-10 ESV

"Blessed are you who are hungry now, for you shall be satisfied." Blessed are you who weep now, for you shall laugh.
Luke 6:21 ESV

Charge them that are rich in this world, that they be not high minded, nor trust in uncertain riches, but in the living God, who giveth us richly all things to enjoy;
1 Timothy 6:17 KJV

Chapter 10
The 1st Water Sprinkler and Shower

By A. Metts. Hope, always hope, even in great downpours! Dance! Expect great things, God can do the impossible!

The 1st Water Sprinkler and Shower!

Wouldn't you know it! God made the first water sprinkler. His perfectly rhythmed rain is the drink of nearly every living thing on earth. Nations dance in His amazing free thirst quenching droplets! He created the first shower to wash away unsightly dirt. Life on earth would die swiftly without His sprinkler. Bodies of water would dry up without His refilling. God's sprinkler operates at several speeds. He offers the mist, the light rain, the heavy rain, the torrential downpour, or even the hurricane strength spray. Here again, He is found to be so generous. Matthew 5:45 tells us that God causes it to rain on the just and the unjust. This means that God gives rain to those who know Him and to those who do not know Him. I love His generosity. He knows Who He is whether a person acknowledges Him or not. There is no god like Him!

During the next storm, allow the rain kiss your face. Feel the thousand tiny gifts as they unwrap upon you. Dance through the puddles splashing and making great fun. Only if there is NO lightning! LOL! Just know every drop is a gift from heaven. His rain washes away unnecessary things. His rain forces the unseen seed to yield to the seen. His rain brings great harvests. His rain washes the dust from our weary souls. His rain refreshes us all. Thank You Father for Your rain!

So that you may be sons of your Father in heaven; for He makes His sun to rise on the evil and on the good, and sends rain on the just and the unjust.
Matthew 5:45 ESV

Yet He did not leave Himself without witness, for He did good by giving you rains from heaven and fruitful seasons, satisfying our hearts with food and gladness."
Acts 14:17 ESV

The 1st Water Sprinkler and Shower

"You heavens above rain down my righteousness; let the clouds shower it down. Let the earth open wide, let salvation spring up, let righteousness flourish with it; I, the LORD, have created it.

Isaiah 45:8 NIV

Chapter 11
The 1st Fan

By J. Metts. Myself, playing in God's wind!

The 1ˢᵗ Fan

Absolutely, God made the first fan! His refreshing wind has blown from the dawn of creation. Complete with an invisible motor this wind has cooled us all. This great economic fan blows without electricity. This fan knows no boundaries and no race. It is generous to all, great or small! God's brilliant fan blows dead leaves from trees in fall or tosses old limbs great or small. It blows sand into great hills or snow into massive mounds. His wind tosses the greatest of waves or pushes the largest of ships. His fan cools the hot laborer. His fan directs the weather and drives the rain. It can break ships in half, and toss terrible waves. His fan often blows hats off unexpectedly or may move a woman's dress like that of a perfect dance. His fan is invisible, unpredictable, soft, powerful, and without cord or shut off. His fan can gently blow across the face a crying baby or forcefully upon an entire nation. God in His magnificence has created something so huge yet so tender. This invisible powerful wind produces profound evidence of its invisible presence.

> He who forms the mountains, who creates the wind, and who reveals his thoughts to mankind, who turns dawn to darkness, and treads on the heights of the earth ~ the LORD God Almighty is his name. Amos 4:13 NIV

> God is Spirit: and those who worship Him must worship Him in spirit and truth. John 4:24 NKJV

Often I have heard the Spirit of God is much like the wind. You cannot see Him but He is there. The evidence of Him shouts through all His creation and blows through those who invite Him into their life. Just as the wind blows and moves great limbs and leaves, even so the Lord's Spirit flows through His people directing and helping them to do things they could never do in their own strength, like helping me write this book. I was deeply moved when I read Colossians chapter one verse fifteen. This verse is talking about Jesus Christ.

> He (JESUS) is the image of the invisible God, the firstborn of all creation. Colossians 1:15 ESV

When we want to see what God looks like in the physical form, we can study the life of Jesus. He carried all authority yet clothed Himself in the royal cloth of humility. He died and rose to life that we may come back to our Father! Never have I met any person on earth who longs more for our victory in life than Jesus does! He stays closer than a brother. Jesus could have at any time given Himself over to doubt, sorrow, hatred or even revenge yet He stayed faithful to the very will and heart of God. Jesus overcame evil with good. He gave His sinless life to pay for the world's sin so that if they choose to come to the Father they could. It was for the great joy of reuniting us to our Father that He willingly laid down His life. The more I learn about Jesus the more I love God and Him. How beautiful God truly is! I love You Jesus! Thank You!!!

"For God so loved the world, that He gave His only Son, that whoever believes in Him should not perish but have eternal life. John 3:16 ESV

Chapter 12
The 1st Rainbow

By A. Metts. This picture of the rainbow I took on a mission trip in New Mexico. I love God's promises!

The 1st Rainbow

The rainbow has caused us to stare in reverent awe for generations. God's radiant art again on display! Rainbows form when the sunlight shines through water. Light bends and reflects causing seven brilliant colors to appear; red, orange, yellow, green, blue, and indigo. A rainbow brightens the most questionable sky. The first rainbow is recorded in the book of Genesis as a sign of God's promise to all generations. All generations includes the previous generations, you and every person after you. God made this promise after He flooded the entire earth.

The LORD saw that the wickedness of man was great in the earth, and that every intention of the thoughts of his heart was only evil continually. And the Lord regretted that He had made man on the earth, and it grieved Him to His heart. Genesis 6:5-6 ESV

God has a heart! His heart was so grieved because of the evil He saw mankind (mankind includes both men and woman) doing on the earth. Whether a person believes God sees what they do or not....it is clear that God sees everything we do! He then looked inside of man and found even man's thoughts were evil. Thoughts are the first step to a person's actions. God knew they would do more and more evil. God regretted that He made man, and it grieved Him to His heart. He was grieved to the very core... so deep. He sent the flood to drown everyone and everything except Noah, his family and the animals God commanded him to load on the Ark. Who knew God's heart could be so grieved. It touches my own heart to know He looked even closer at the inside of man to see if there might be any good thoughts. It is so sad He did not find good thoughts, may He find good thoughts in us.

> *And God said, "This is the sign of the covenant that I make between me and you and every living creature that is with you, for all future generations: I have set My rainbow in the cloud, and it shall be a sign of the covenant between me and the earth. When I bring clouds over the earth and the rainbow is seen in the clouds, I will remember My covenant that is between Me and you and every living creature of all flesh. And the waters shall never again become a flood to destroy all flesh. Genesis 9:12-15 ESV*

God says several times when He sees His rainbow that He Himself would remember His own promise never to flood the entire earth again. He created the promising rainbow not only for us but Himself. He reminds us after great storms that His promise is still true. Even after so many, many years. He still shines His rainbow! Hope seems to fill our hearts when a rainbow appears. Hope that whatever storm we may be facing we have an amazing God who cares. Unlike so many people who break their word or promise, God has never broken a promise. He is God; there is no weakness in Him.

My longing is that we all might learn from His perfect example and keep our own promises. Let us not allow ourselves to make promises without thinking them through or counting the cost. We should remind ourselves of the promises we have made just as the Lord does. We can ask Him to empower us to keep these promises. If we fail, may we quickly apologize and make all amends necessary. There are times we are the poorest representation of Him. Let us we be quick to repent and do right.

> If a man vows a vow to the LORD, or swears and oath to bind himself by a pledge, he shall not break his word. He shall do according to all that proceeds out of his mouth.
> Numbers 30:2 ESV

> God is not man, that He should lie, or a son of man, that He should change His mind. Has He said, and will He not do it? Or has He spoken, and will He not fulfill it? Numbers 23:19 ESV

> Let what you say be simply 'Yes' or 'No'; anything more than this comes from evil. Matthew 5:37 ESV

Psalm 104

1. Bless the LORD, O my soul! O LORD, my God, You are very great! You are clothed with splendor and majesty,
2. Covering Yourself with light as with a garment, Stretching out the heavens like a tent.
3. He lays the beams of His chambers on the waters; He makes the clouds His chariot; He rides on the wings of the wind;
4. He makes His messengers winds, His ministers a flaming fire.
5. He set the earth on its foundations, so that it should never be moved.
6. You covered it with the deep as with a garment; the waters stood above the mountains.
7. At Your rebuke they fled; at the sound of Your thunder they took to flight.
8. The mountains rose, the valleys sank down to the place that You appointed for them.
9. You set a boundary that they may not pass, so that they might not again cover the earth.
10. You make springs gush forth in the valleys; they flow between the hills;
11. They give drink to every beast of the field; the wild donkeys quench their thirst.

12. Beside them the birds of the heavens dwell; they sing among the branches.

13. From Your lofty abode You water the mountains; the earth is satisfied with the fruit of Your work.

14. You cause the grass to grow for the livestock and plants for man to cultivate, that he may bring forth food from the earth

15. And wine to gladden the heart of man, oil to make his face shine and bread to strengthen man's heart.

16. The trees of the LORD are watered abundantly, the cedars of Lebanon that He planted.

17. In them the birds build their nests; the stork has her home in the fir trees.

18. The high mountains are for the wild goats; the rocks are a refuge for the rock badgers.

19. He made the moon to mark the seasons; the sun knows its time for setting.

20. You make darkness, and it is night, when all the beasts of the forest creep about.

21. The young lions roar for their prey, seeking their food from God.

22. When the sun rises, they steal away and lie down in their dens.

23. Man goes out to his work and to his labor until the evening.

24. O LORD, how manifold are Your works! In wisdom You have made them all; the earth is full of Your creatures.

25. Here is the sea, great and wide, which teems with creatures innumerable, living things both small and great.

26. There go the ships, and Leviathan, which You formed to play in it.

27. These all look to You, to give them their food in due season.

28. When You give it to them they gather it up; when You open Your hand, they are filled with good things.

29. When You hide Your face, they are dismayed; when You take away their breath, they die and return to their dust.

30. When You send forth Your Spirit, they are created, and You renew the face of the ground.

31. May the glory of the LORD endure forever; may the LORD rejoice in His works,

32. Who looks on the earth and it trembles, Who touches the mountains and they smoke!

33. I will sing to the LORD as long as I live; I will sing praise to my God while I have my being.

34. May my meditation be pleasing to Him, for I rejoice in the LORD.

35. Let sinners be consumed from the earth, and let the wicked be not more! Bless the LORD, O my soul! Praise the LORD! ESV

Psalm 104

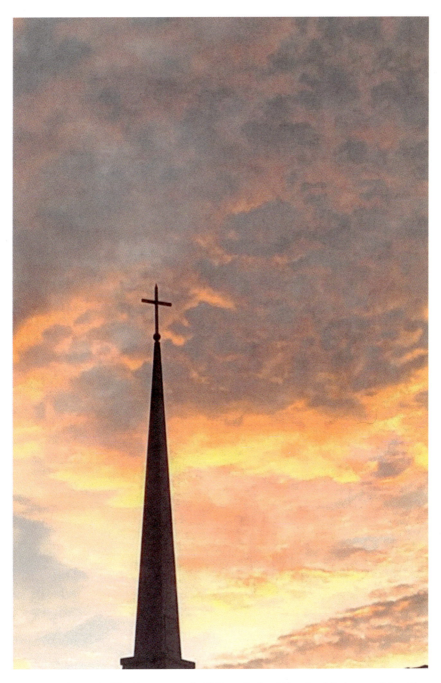

By A. Metts. God's glory revealed! Reach for Him for He is reaching for you!

~Closing~

This book is but a very small example of the greatness of God. I hope in reading it you have found His overwhelming faithful love. For He exceeds our greatest expectation! Dare to seek Him...Dare to feel for Him...you will find Him, He promised. He is the greatest treasure ever to be sought, and the very reason for our lives!

Always, in His love, Angela

You may contact the author at the following email or address.

Ametts2016@gmail.com

Angela Metts

P.O. Box 878

Cleveland Texas 77328

~Closing~

Treasures...for your journey...

* He promises to reward you when you seek Him. (Hebrews 11:6)
* God is love! 1st John 4:8, Romans 5:8, 1st John 3:1
* God made us in His image! Genesis 1:27
* God feeds the birds! Matthew 6:26
* God sings over His people! Zephaniah 3:17
* God knows your thoughts and where you go! Psalm 139
* Cry out for God, He will hear you. Psalm 77:10
* Nothing and no one can take Gods love from you. Romans 8:38-39
* God loved you so much He sent His son to save you. John 3:16
* Jesus can save you! Romans 10:9-10
* God can wash away your sins! 1st John 1:9
* Jesus (God's Son) cooked fish! John 21:1-14
* God promised never to leave you! Hebrews 13:5
* Believe in Jesus and receive eternal life! John 3:16
* God does not want you to be afraid! Isaiah 41:10, 2nd Timothy 1:7
* God is our strength and help. Psalm 46:1-3
* God can meet your needs! Philippians 4:19
* God can heal you! Exodus 15:26, Isaiah 53:5
* People in the world hated God first. John 15:18, Luke 6:22, 2 Timothy 3:12
* Jesus will come back to earth! Revelation 22:12-13, John 14:3

Made in the USA
Coppell, TX
10 November 2022